# EIFFEL TOWER

## Bryan Pezzi

www.av2books.com

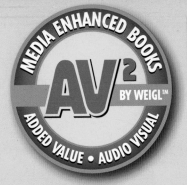

AV² provides enriched content that supplements and complements this book. Weigl's AV² books strive to create inspired learning and engage young minds in a total learning experience.

## Your AV² Media Enhanced books come alive with...

**Audio**
Listen to sections of the book read aloud.

**Key Words**
Study vocabulary, and complete a matching word activity.

**Video**
Watch informative video clips.

**Quizzes**
Test your knowledge.

**Embedded Weblinks**
Gain additional information for research.

**Slide Show**
View images and captions, and prepare a presentation.

Go to **www.av2books.com**, and enter this book's unique code.

**BOOK CODE**

M 4 8 1 8 0 0

AV² by Weigl brings you media enhanced books that support active learning.

**Try This!**
Complete activities and hands-on experiments.

**... and much, much more!**

---

Published by AV² by Weigl
350 5th Avenue, 59th Floor
New York, NY 10118
Website: www.av2books.com    www.weigl.com

Library of Congress Cataloging-in-Publication
Pezzi, Bryan.
  Eiffel Tower / Bryan Pezzi and Heather Kissock.
    p. cm. -- (Virtual field trips)
  Includes index.
  ISBN 978-1-61690-766-2 (hardcover : alk. paper) -- ISBN 978-1-61690-770-9 (pbk. : alk. paper) -- ISBN 978-1-61690-433-3 (online)
  1.  Tour Eiffel (Paris, France)--Juvenile literature. 2.  Civil engineering--France--Paris--History--Juvenile literature. 3.  Eiffel, Gustave, 1832-1923--Juvenile literature. I. Kissock, Heather. II. Title.
  TA149.P493 2012
  725'.97094436--dc23
                    2011019312

Printed in the United States of America in North Mankato, Minnesota
1 2 3 4 5 6 7 8 9 0  15 14 13 12 11

052011
WEP290411

Editor: Heather Kissock
Design: Terry Paulhus

Every reasonable effort has been made to trace ownership and to obtain permission to reprint copyright material. The publishers would be pleased to have any errors or omission brought to their attention so that they may be corrected in subsequent printings.

Weigl acknowledges Getty Images as its primary image supplier for this title.

# Contents

# What is the Eiffel Tower?

Some structures are known throughout the world. The Eiffel Tower is one such structure. It stands as a symbol of Paris, France. This massive structure was built for the Paris Centennial **Exposition** that was held in the city in 1889. During this time, the **Industrial Revolution** was changing how people lived and worked. The Eiffel Tower was an example of these changes. It was different from any structure built before. A better understanding of science allowed people to build in new ways.

The Eiffel Tower was built by a French engineer named Alexandre-Gustave Eiffel. At 1,024 feet (312 meters) high, it was taller than any other structure at the time. The previous record holder, the Washington Monument, was only 555 feet (169 m). One of the reasons Eiffel's tower could reach such a great height was Eiffel's use of building materials. While the Washington Monument was made of heavy stone, the Eiffel Tower was built of iron. Metal was replacing wood and stone as a popular building material. It was strong and light, and it could be produced more cheaply.

Parisians thought the large, metal Eiffel Tower looked unusual. Some thought it destroyed the city's beauty. Today, it is difficult to imagine Paris without this structure.

About 230 million people have visited the Eiffel Tower since it was built.

# Snapshot of France

Covering 210,026 square miles (543,965 square kilometers), France is western Europe's largest country. It shares its eastern borders with Belgium, Luxembourg, Germany, Switzerland, and Italy. Spain sits along its southwest border. To its west are the waters of the Bay of Biscay and the English Channel. The Mediterranean Sea is found along France's southeast coast.

## INTRODUCING FRANCE

**CAPITAL CITY:** Paris

**FLAG:**

**POPULATION:** 62,814,233 (2011)

**OFFICIAL LANGUAGE:** French

**CURRENCY:** Euro

**CLIMATE:** Cool winters and mild summers, warmer along the Mediterranean

**SUMMER TEMPERATURE:** Average of 77° Fahrenheit (25° Celsius)

**WINTER TEMPERATURE:** Average of 34°F (1°C)

**TIME ZONE:** Central European Time (CET)

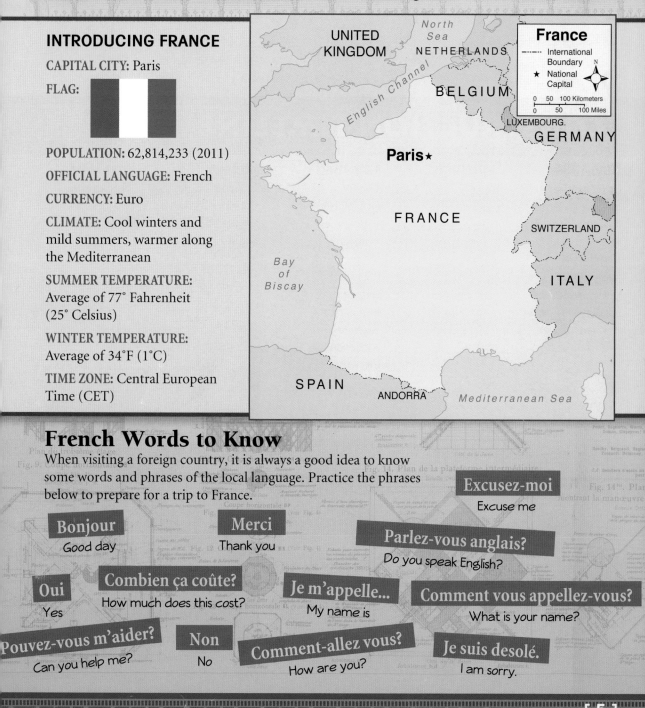

## French Words to Know

When visiting a foreign country, it is always a good idea to know some words and phrases of the local language. Practice the phrases below to prepare for a trip to France.

**Excusez-moi**
Excuse me

**Bonjour**
Good day

**Merci**
Thank you

**Parlez-vous anglais?**
Do you speak English?

**Oui**
Yes

**Combien ça coûte?**
How much does this cost?

**Je m'appelle...**
My name is

**Comment vous appellez-vous?**
What is your name?

**Pouvez-vous m'aider?**
Can you help me?

**Non**
No

**Comment-allez vous?**
How are you?

**Je suis desolé.**
I am sorry.

# A Step Back in Time

In the late 1800s, France went through a period known as the *Belle Epoque*, or the "beautiful era." After years of war and hardship, France was enjoying a time of peace and prosperity. The development of new industries had led to greater wealth for the French, and they wanted to show the world that France was a great power.

## CONSTRUCTION TIMELINE

### June 1884
Eiffel's chief engineers, Emile Nouguier and Maurice Koechlin, present the initial design for a 1,000-foot (305-m) tower to Eiffel.

### September 1884
Eiffel registers a patent for a metal structure that can exceed 1,000 feet (305 m).

### May 1886
The French government announces a design competition for the 1889 Centennial Exposition. Gustave Eiffel is chosen as the winner.

### January 1887
**Excavation** of the Eiffel Tower's proposed site begins.

### June 1887
The Eiffel Tower's **foundation** is in place.

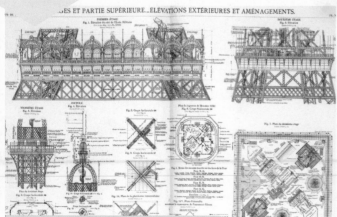

Gustave Eiffel included drawings of the Eiffel Tower in his book, *The 300-Meter Tower*.

The Eiffel Tower's foundations were built in five months.

The government planned a great exposition for 1889. Its purpose was to show the technological advances that France had made. The planners wanted to find a symbol for this event. They decided a great metal tower should be built. The government held a contest to choose a design. More than 100 people submitted entries. Gustave Eiffel, a French engineer, was the winner. Eiffel was known for his innovative use of metal in bridges and other structures.

The Eiffel Tower drew about 12,000 visitors each day of the exposition.

**July 1, 1887**
Construction begins on the Eiffel Tower.

**April 1888**
The first of three levels is completed.

**August 1888**
The second level is completed.

**March 31, 1889**
The Eiffel Tower is completed, almost two months ahead of schedule.

**May 6, 1889**
The Paris Centennial Exposition opens.

The metal pieces of the Eiffel Tower took 21 months to assemble.

# The Eiffel Tower Location

The Eiffel Tower is located on the Champ de Mars, on the left bank of the Seine River, in Paris, France. The Champ de Mars is a long strip of land that was used as a parade square for a nearby military school. The area covers about 60 acres (24.5 hectares).

The Champ de Mars has been the location of all of the **World's Fairs** held in Paris since 1867. Due to its expanse of land, it has been used for gatherings and celebrations since at least the 1700s.

The Eiffel Tower remains the focal point of the Champ de Mars, and of Paris itself.

# The Eiffel Tower Today

Today, the Eiffel Tower stands 39 feet (12 m) higher than when it was constructed. A radio antenna was added to the top of the tower in 1957, increasing its height. About six million people visit the Eiffel Tower every year.

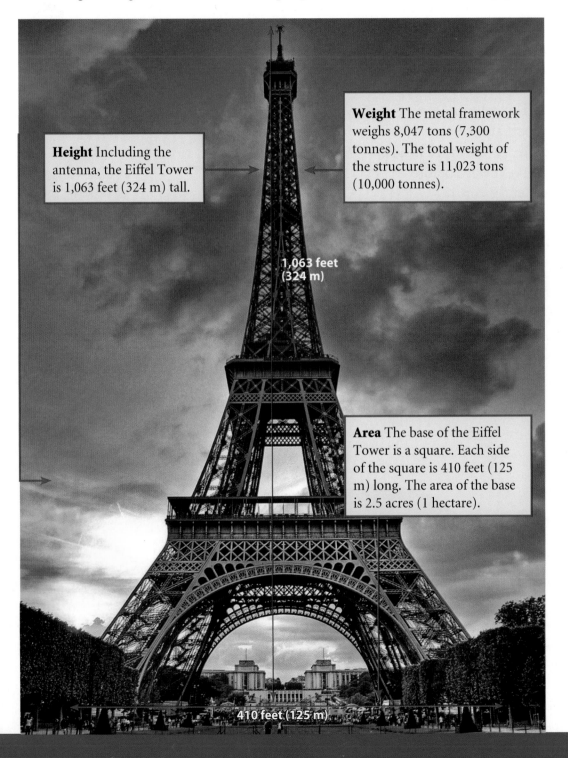

**Height** Including the antenna, the Eiffel Tower is 1,063 feet (324 m) tall.

**Weight** The metal framework weighs 8,047 tons (7,300 tonnes). The total weight of the structure is 11,023 tons (10,000 tonnes).

1,063 feet (324 m)

**Area** The base of the Eiffel Tower is a square. Each side of the square is 410 feet (125 m) long. The area of the base is 2.5 acres (1 hectare).

410 feet (125 m)

# Outside the Eiffel Tower

*The Eiffel Tower is best known for its exterior. Its decorative ironwork and soaring height make it one of the best-known structures in the world.*

**Columns** The key components of the tower are the four columns of metal **girders** that form its triangular shape. The columns are set wide apart at the base of the structure. As they gain height, they curve inward before joining at the top.

Each of the tower's four columns, or legs, is made up of four columns as well.

Arches are often used to support the upper parts of a structure.

**Arches** Four giant arches sweep across the base of the tower, connecting the legs together. The arches provide support to the upper parts of the tower. They support the tower's weight by converting the downward force of its weight into an outward force. This means that the arches help transfer the weight from the top of the tower to the four metal columns at the base.

The openness of the lattice pattern allows visitors to stand in one part of the tower and look through to another part.

**Lattice Pattern** Much of the metal that makes up the Eiffel Tower has been put together in a lattice pattern. This is a pattern made up of triangles, with at least two ends connecting to the main frame of the structure. As the pattern is formed by metal strips, the tower has an open, airy appearance.

**Paint** The Eiffel Tower is painted every seven years. Currently, the tower is painted bronze. Different shades of this color are used on each level. The paint is a dark shade on the bottom. Each level is lighter in shade. This makes the tower appear taller. About 55 tons (50 tonnes) of paint are required to paint the tower.

The Eiffel Tower has changed color six times since it was built.

Twenty thousand light bulbs are used to illuminate the tower. Each side of the tower has 5,000 lights.

# VIRTUAL TOUR

For 40 years, the Eiffel Tower was the world's tallest structure. It lost this title when the Chrysler Building was built in New York City in 1930.

**Lights** Paris is often called "The City of Lights." The Eiffel Tower helps the city earn this reputation with its many light bulbs. Every evening, the tower's 20,000 bulbs light up for five minutes every hour on the hour, creating a sparkling monument over the city.

# Inside the Eiffel Tower

*The Eiffel Tower was always meant to be a place for people to visit. Its interior was created for Parisians and tourists alike.*

**Platforms** Each of the Eiffel Tower's three levels allows visitors a spectacular view of Paris. The first level platform is 187 feet (57 m) from the ground. The second level is 377 feet (115 m) high. The third level is found at a height of 906 feet (276 m). People can access the first two levels by either stairs or elevators. The third level can be reached only by elevator.

On a clear day, the view from the tower's top level can reach 45 miles (72 kilometers).

The Eiffel Tower was one of the first structures to include passenger elevators.

**Elevators** When building the tower, Eiffel included a system of elevators to move visitors between the different levels. These elevators do not run straight up and down. Instead, they follow the path of the tower's curved and angled legs. Three elevators run from the ground level to the first and second platforms. Another elevator takes visitors from the second platform to the top of the tower.

## Gustave Eiffel's Office

The top level of the tower is home to Gustave Eiffel's office. The room has been restored to its original condition and contains mementos from the tower's construction. There is even a wax figure of Eiffel himself sitting at his desk.

The scene in the office recreates a meeting between Gustave Eiffel and U.S. inventor Thomas Edison. Eiffel's daughter stands in the background.

The Eiffel Tower's restaurants offer visitors a unique view of the city.

**Restaurants** When it was first built, the Eiffel Tower had four restaurants on its first level. This was later reduced to two. Today, the first level has one restaurant. In 1983, a restaurant was built on the second level for the first time. Still in operation today, it serves gourmet food and is serviced by its own elevator.

**Stairways** People who want to get some exercise have the option of using the stairs instead of the elevators. The stairways take people all the way from the ground to the second level. When the tower was built, a winding staircase led to the top level. However, this staircase has now been replaced with an elevator.

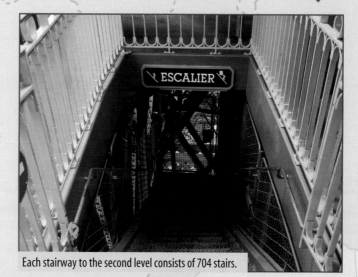

Each stairway to the second level consists of 704 stairs.

# Big Ideas Behind the Eiffel Tower

Gustave Eiffel knew that the use of metal would allow him to build big structures. He had used iron in his own previous designs for bridges and **viaducts**. Eiffel knew that the same kind of metalwork could be used in a monumental structure, such as a very high tower.

## The Properties of Iron

When the Industrial Revolution began in Europe, metal became widely used as a building material. **Wrought iron**, **cast iron**, and steel were common. Of the three, wrought iron is the heaviest and is unlikely to buckle. It is easy to work with and strong enough to withstand the weather conditions. Cast iron is weaker and more brittle than wrought iron or steel. At the time, steel was fairly new and expensive. It was lighter than iron, but not as strong. After considering the options, Eiffel chose to build his tower out of wrought iron. It was the most practical material because of its strength, flexibility, and durability. Wrought iron was also available at reasonable costs.

As an engineer, Eiffel needed to know the characteristics of different metals. This allowed him to choose the material that best suited the structure being built.

## Withstanding Wind

In building the world's tallest structure, Eiffel's biggest challenge was to make the tower able to withstand the force of wind. He designed the columns of the tower to curve inward. Through mathematical calculations, Eiffel knew that this was the best shape to withstand wind pressure. He built the tower not as one large solid, but as a network of crisscrossed iron beams. There are large

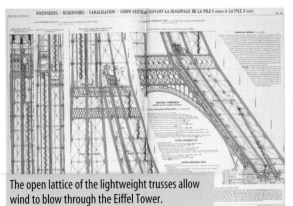

The open lattice of the lightweight trusses allow wind to blow through the Eiffel Tower.

amounts of empty space between the beams, so wind can easily pass through. Eiffel's design ensures the tower can withstand even the strongest Paris winds.

# Science at Work at the Eiffel Tower

Eiffel had a strong background in science. In order to build a structure like the Eiffel Tower, he needed to understand all the scientific principles at work.

Creeper cranes have been used to build a number of structures, from towers to bridges.

## Creeper Cranes

Cranes are useful in the construction of many structures. They are tall machines with long arms used for moving objects. Cranes can lift metal beams, large tools, and other heavy objects. The Eiffel Tower was such a tall structure that the workers needed an efficient way to lift materials to the upper levels. Eiffel used a special kind of crane for this task. Creeper cranes were small, steam-powered cranes. They were mounted onto sloping tracks that crept up the columns of the tower. Without creeper cranes, there would have been no way to move materials to such great heights. The 13-ton (11.8-tonne) cranes could pivot a full 360 degrees and move up the tracks as the tower's construction progressed.

## Hydraulics

Many early machines, such as creeper cranes, were operated by steam power. At the time of the Eiffel Tower's construction, a new, more efficient technology was developing. **Hydraulics** is a system that powers many of the machines on today's construction sites,

Hydraulic systems use liquid to transmit force, allowing hydraulic lifts to easily haul thousands of pounds.

including bulldozers and forklifts. A hydraulic system uses two pistons in cylinders filled with an incompressible oil. This is oil that cannot be squeezed into a smaller space. The cylinders are connected by a pipe, which may be any length or shape. When force is applied to one of the pistons, the force is transmitted to the second piston through the oil in the pipe.

## VIRTUAL TOUR

On a windy day, the top of the Eiffel Tower only sways up to 2.75 inches (7 centimeters) in any direction.

# The Eiffel Tower Builders

Although Gustav Eiffel was responsible for the creation of the Eiffel Tower, there were many others involved in building the structure. Among them were ironworkers, glaziers, and crane operators.

Eiffel was born in 1832 in Dijon, France. He died in 1923 at the age of 91.

## Alexandre-Gustave Eiffel

### Chief Engineer

After graduating from the École Centrale des Arts et Manufactures, one of Europe's top engineering schools, Eiffel took a job with an engineering firm. He quickly earned a reputation as an efficient builder who used innovative techniques. He started his own business in 1864, opening metalwork shops northwest of Paris. Eiffel became known as the "magician of iron." His technique of crisscrossing iron beams to give a webbed appearance became his trademark style. From 1867 to 1885, Eiffel's company built 42 railway bridges and viaducts. One of Eiffel's projects was the Statue of Liberty. However, it was the Eiffel Tower that became the highlight of his career. After it was built, Eiffel's name became known throughout the world.

The Eiffel Tower's arches originally served as an entrance to the Paris Exposition.

## Stephen Sauvestre Architect

Eiffel hired an architect named Stephen Sauvestre to work on the tower's appearance. Sauvestre planned the large arches that stretch between the legs of the tower. These design elements give the tower its distinctive appearance.

## Emile Nouguier and Maurice Koechlin Engineers

Emile Nouguier and Maurice Koechlin were engineers in Eiffel's company. They played a key role in the early planning stages of the tower. The two men had been working on the idea of a tall tower for many years. Their plan was to have four large columns made up of metal girders.

The columns would curve inward and join together at the top. Three platforms at different levels would allow visitors a spectacular view of the city.

Although the tower is named after Gustave Eiffel, the structural concept of the four columns originated with Nouguier and Koechlin.

More than a century later, ironworkers are still needed to put up buildings, bridges, and other structures.

## Welders

Welders apply heat to melt and fuse metal pieces together. Working with heat and fire can be dangerous, so welders need to take special precautions. They must wear heavy gloves, long-sleeved jackets, and eye protection. Workers must be physically fit, have good coordination, and be able to focus on the job at hand.

Some welders work in unusual places, such as atop skyscrapers, under water, or even in outer space.

## Ironworkers

Ironworkers played a critical role in the construction of the Eiffel Tower. Ironworkers read **blueprints** and install the metal parts of a structure. They set up the framework of a building and bolt the metal pieces into place. Sometimes, ironworkers are responsible for tasks such as reinforcing concrete with metal bars. They might also work on metal railings or stairwells. Ironworkers need to be in good physical condition. They must have good mechanical skills and be handy with tools. Ironworkers must always follow proper safety procedures to avoid injury on a construction site.

## Glaziers

Glaziers are people who install the glass parts in structures. Usually, glass is cut at a factory. It is then moved to a construction site where a glazier installs it. Glaziers use many tools, such as knives, suction cups, glass grinders, saws, and drills. The job may require lifting heavy glass panels or working at great heights. Glaziers must be careful to avoid injuries caused by broken glass.

Using glass as a building material became popular in the 1800s. Today, glass is used in the construction of a variety of structures, including homes, offices, and skyscrapers.

# Similar Structures Around the World

The 1800s were a time of change for builders and architects. The Industrial Revolution allowed people to **mass-produce** new kinds of building materials, such as metal and glass. A new style of building emerged in Europe and the United States at this time. These structures could be very large and strong. At the same time, they could let in large amounts of light. The effect was a taller, lighter, and brighter space. The Eiffel Tower was only one of the many unique structures built in this style.

## The Crystal Palace Exhibition Hall

**BUILT:** 1851
**LOCATION:** London, England
**DESIGN:** Sir Joseph Paxton, architect
**DESCRIPTION:** This giant hall was an intricate network of thin iron rods and sheets of clear glass. It was built as an exhibition space for London's Great Exhibition of 1851. The building's main body was 1,851 feet (564 m) long and 456 feet (139 m) wide.

The Auditorium Theatre has played host to all sorts of events, ranging from political conventions to operas.

During London's Great Exhibition, more than 14,000 exhibitors came to the Crystal Palace to showcase their new technology.

## Auditorium Theatre

**BUILT:** 1889
**LOCATION:** Chicago, Illinois
**DESIGN:** Louis Sullivan, architect; Dankmar Adler, engineer
**DESCRIPTION:** The Auditorium Theatre was the tallest building in Chicago at the time. It was built using modern technology, such as lighting and air conditioning. Today, the building is a National Historic Landmark. It has 24-karat, gold-leafed ceilings and detailed stencil patterns and murals throughout.

## Bon Marché

**BUILT:** 1876
**LOCATION:** Paris, France
**DESIGN:** Louis-Auguste Boileau, architect; Gustave Eiffel, engineer
**DESCRIPTION:** The Bon Marché was the world's first true department store. In 1876, the store moved into a new building. Engineered by Gustave Eiffel, the structure was built of iron and glass. Skylights in the ceiling allowed light to shine on interior courts.

The Bon Marché began as a small corner shop and grew into one of the world's foremost department stores.

## St. Pancras Station

**BUILT:** 1868
**LOCATION:** London, England
**DESIGN:** William Henry Barlow, engineer
**DESCRIPTION:** St. Pancras is known as one of the great Victorian-era train stations. The building's train shed has an iron frame roof, which spans a distance of 243 feet (74 m). This huge enclosed space and the transparent iron framework looked futuristic to people of the 19th century.

When it was completed in 1868, St. Pancras Station's train shed became the largest enclosed space in the world.

# Issues Facing the Tower

During the Industrial Revolution, the focus was on technology and mass production. People did not pay much attention to the effects this technology had on the environment. Today, the people managing the Eiffel Tower have to consider how the tower affects the environment and how the environment affects the tower.

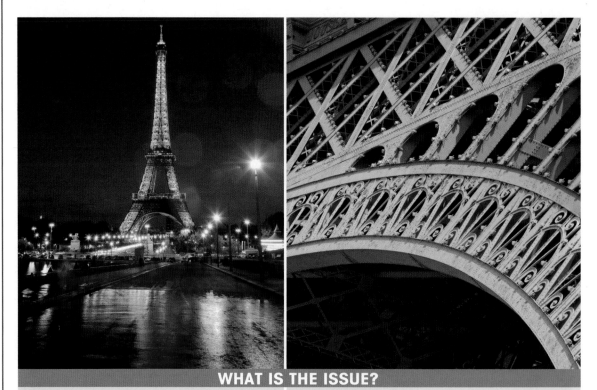

## WHAT IS THE ISSUE?

The Eiffel Tower is a huge consumer of energy. It uses 7,000 megawatts every hour. Six percent of this energy is used just for lighting.

Exposure to rain, snow, and wind causes metal to rust and corrode. This damage is called weathering.

## EFFECTS

Excessive energy consumption drains resources and can contribute to **global warming**.

**Corrosion**, in the form of rust, eats away at the metal, creating holes. This can affect the safety of the structure.

## ACTION TAKEN

The tower has a contract with its energy supplier guaranteeing that all of its energy must come from 100 percent **renewable energy** sources. Lower-energy bulbs are also used.

Every seven years, the tower is painted. To prepare the metal, corroded areas are sanded down and cleaned. Paint is then applied to the metal. The paint protects the tower from further damage.

# Create a Support Beam

Gustave Eiffel was an expert at building structures out of metal beams. A beam is a piece of material that resists bending. The shape of a beam can affect how strong it is. Using stiff paper or cardboard, create beams in different shapes, and test each beam to find out how strong it is.

## Materials
- several sheets of light cardboard or stiff construction paper
- tape
- two piles of books
- weights, such as standard metal weights, marbles, or weights made out of modeling clay

## Instructions

1. Fold or bend the paper to create beams in different shapes. Use tape to hold the beams in shape. Try the following shapes.

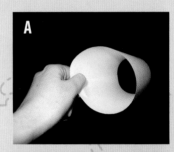

   a. Bend one sheet of paper to create a hollow, circular beam. It will be cylindrical in shape.

   b. Fold one sheet three times lengthwise, and then fold together to create a square beam.

   c. Fold one sheet twice lengthwise, and then fold together to create a triangular beam.

   d. Fold one sheet several times lengthwise to create an accordion-pattern beam.

2. Create two piles of books of equal height, with a gap between the two piles.

3. Bridge the gap between the book piles with a flat piece of paper first. Add weight to the paper until it collapses. Record how much weight was needed to collapse the paper.

4. Try each of the beams. Again, record how much weight can be added before the beam collapses. You might need to hang the weights underneath, depending on the shape of the beam.

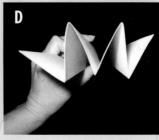

5. Record data for each of the beams, and determine which of the beams supports the most weight.

# Eiffel Tower Quiz

**Q** What kind of metal was used to build the Eiffel Tower?

**A** The Eiffel Tower was made from wrought iron.

**Q** Why was the Eiffel Tower built?

**A** The Eiffel Tower was built for the Paris Centennial Exposition of 1889. It was to showcase the technological advances that France had made in recent years.

**Q** What other famous structure was Gustave Eiffel responsible for building?

**A** The Statue of Liberty.

**Q** How often is the Eiffel Tower painted?

**A** Every seven years.

# Glossary

**blueprints:** prints of plans used to build structures

**cast iron:** iron containing so much carbon that it cannot be shaped by hammering, rolling, or pressing. It must be poured into a mold to create a shape.

**corrosion:** the act of eating or wearing away gradually, especially by chemical action

**excavation:** the removal of soil and earth to make a hole in which a structure can be built

**exposition:** a large fair with many exhibits

**foundation:** construction below the ground that distributes the load of a building or other structure built on top of it

**girders:** large iron or steel beams

**global warming:** an increase in the average temperature of Earth's atmosphere

**hydraulics:** machines that use liquid pressure to enable a small force applied to one piston to produce force on another piston

**Industrial Revolution:** a period in European history that was characterized by the development of industry on a wide scale

**mass-produce:** to manufacture items to a standardized pattern in huge quantities

**renewable energy:** an energy resource that is replaced rapidly by natural processes

**viaducts:** long, bridgelike structures that carry a road or railroad over a valley

**World's Fairs:** international expositions featuring exhibits and participants from all over the world

**wrought iron:** a pure form of iron having low carbon content; often used for decorative work

# Index

# Log on to www.av2books.com

AV² by Weigl brings you media enhanced books that support active learning. Go to www.av2books.com, and enter the special code found on page 2 of this book. You will gain access to enriched and enhanced content that supplements and complements this book. Content includes video, audio, web links, quizzes, a slide show, and activities.

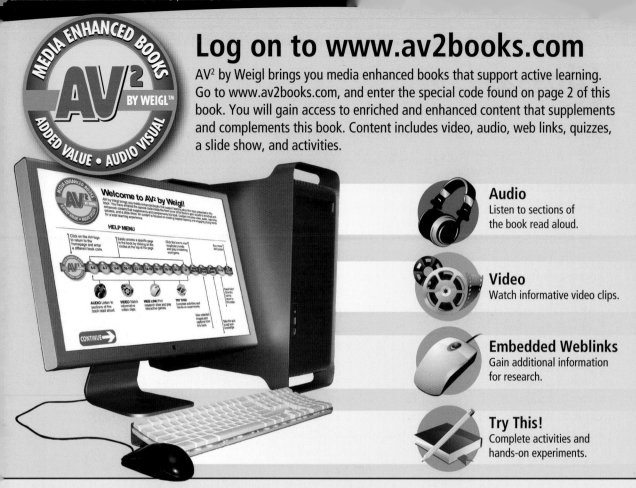

**Audio**
Listen to sections of the book read aloud.

**Video**
Watch informative video clips.

**Embedded Weblinks**
Gain additional information for research.

**Try This!**
Complete activities and hands-on experiments.

# WHAT'S ONLINE?

| Try This! | Embedded Weblinks | Video | EXTRA FEATURES |
|---|---|---|---|
| Test your knowledge of French. | Find out more about where the Eiffel Tower is located. | Watch a video introduction to the Eiffel Tower. | **Audio** Listen to sections of the book read aloud. |
| Test your knowledge of the history of the Eiffel Tower in a timeline activity. | Learn more about a notable person from the history of the Eiffel Tower. | Watch a video about another tour destination near the Eiffel Tower. | **Key Words** Study vocabulary, and complete a matching word activity. |
| Learn more about the math behind the Eiffel Tower. | Learn more about becoming an architect. | | **Slide Show** View images and caption and prepare a presentati |
| Compare modern architects with ancient ones. | Find out more about other important structures near the Eiffel Tower. | | **Quizzes** Test your knowledge. |
| Write about an issue in your community that is similar to one facing the Eiffel Tower. | | | |
| Complete a fun, interactive activity about the Eiffel Tower. | | | |

AV² was built to bridge the gap between print and digital. We encourage you to tell us what you like and what you want to see in the future.

## Sign up to be an AV² Ambassador at www.av2books.com/ambassador.